THE FUN AND EASY WAY TO QUIT SMOKING CIGARETTES FOREVER

NZINGA JOY BURRELL

ISBN: 069244968X
ISBN 13: 9780692449684

Printed in the United States of America

About This Book

This is my first and most meaningful book. It began as an informative report that I wrote in 2012 titled, "The Fun and Easy Way to Quit Cigarettes." After receiving positive feedback from family, friends, and other readers, I decided to extend it into a small book. Why a small book, you ask? Because nobody has less patience than cigarette smokers. I know because I used to be one. When my parents realized I was smoking cigarettes, they gave me a two-hundred-page book on how to quit smoking. I knew after reading about fifteen pages that I would never finish it. It was too long, and I was too impatient then. I had way too many other things to do. Also, it was a rather boring book. It should have been titled *How to Fall Asleep*. So I kept that in mind with this book. I've kept it relatively short and to the point. Therefore, this book is the perfect read for any cigarette smoker. Please give this book to all the smokers you know. It is the perfect, life-enhancing gift.

This book describes the method I used to successfully quit smoking cigarettes forever. To explain this process of quitting cigarettes, I will use a quick analogy of losing weight. Just as there are many ways to lose weight, there are many ways to quit smoking cigarettes. Different ways might work better for different people. Some people may try diet pills, fasting, or extreme fad diets because they might be looking for a quick route. But these people may be harming their health, and then they usually gain the weight back eventually. There is no quick way to lose weight permanently. You must make a permanent mental change, which can take some time. The best way is to adapt to a healthy lifestyle. This includes altering the way you may feel about unhealthy foods and discovering healthy foods and exercises that you enjoy.

When trying to quit smoking cigarettes forever, the concept is very similar. You may have bought nicotine gum or patches, or maybe you even quit cold turkey because you believed it was the best way for you to quit smoking cigarettes. And if you never smoked another one again and know that you never will, then congratulations—because you were right. But if you did smoke a cigarette again, then you must look into making a permanent mental change in the way you feel about cigarettes by changing the way you think and react toward them. You must discover healthier ways to handle stress and healthier ways to experience a natural high. This process may take some time, but it is the most effective way. This method of quitting cigarettes will show you how to do that. It will also teach you to avoid giving in to the temptation to smoke by equipping you with a multilayered defense system. Most importantly, it teaches you how to use a meditative visualization practice to begin preparations before you quit. This will give you a warm-up so that you are mentally stronger for your quit date. The visualization exercises will also strengthen your ability to conquer psychological cigarette cravings. Using the right nicotine therapy and proper usage for physical cigarette cravings, exciting activities to redirect your mind from cigarettes, and fun rewards to motivate your progress, this method packs a powerful punch and will help you conquer even the hardest addiction to cigarettes. This is not a research paper, but I have included some informative data about cigarettes and the tobacco industry. I have also added a few personal stories to bring these methods to life. I have spent a lot of time thoroughly explaining what I did in simple but very detailed terms. Although quitting cigarettes is not easy for most people, this method makes it easier. This book contains one of the smartest and most successful methods of quitting cigarettes. The customizable activities, adventures, and rewards make it very fun. I am very happy to teach it to the world.

The first part of the book is some background and educational information. The second part is the preparation and tools you must gather before your quit date so you can successfully quit. Some tools must be bought and some you must produce in your mind. The third part is for when you actually quit, and the last part includes some helpful final tips.

With this method, I have helped several people quit cigarettes, and I hope that you, or your loved one, are successful at quitting too. Thank you for your purchase, and I welcome any comments that you are willing to take the time to give. Please send any feedback, suggestions, questions, and inquiries for public speaking or book signings to:

QUITSMOKINGCIGARETTES@OUTLOOK.COM

DEDICATION

This book is dedicated to my beautiful and intelligent Auntie Corrine Kagan. As a child, I didn't get to see Auntie Corrine that often because she lived in Los Angeles, but I always knew there was something special about her. And whenever she came to Washington, DC, I'd be extremely happy to see her. She was a nurse, and she always talked about being healthy. Little did I know that years later she would save my life.

I remember it like it was yesterday. I was in sunny Los Angeles visiting her, and we ordered some carry-out. I don't like to ponder why, but it made me sicker than I'd ever been in my entire life. I thought I was going to die. I could barely even move. She gave me a cup of tea, and it took every inch of energy in my body just to turn over. Then I had to summon the strength to reach out and pick up the cup. It took me about two hours to drink that tea in the pretty-little tea cup. That's how sick I was. I wish I remembered the type of tea, but it has been so long. Her kitchen was like an enchanted organic pharmacy, so I'm positive that it was some natural herb that she knew would clean me out.

Fast-forward to several long hours later, and I felt like a new person. I couldn't believe it. I was praising God because it honestly felt like a miracle. She had me up and running the very same day I got sick. Hospitals don't even work that fast. Had I gone to a hospital, I probably would have been there for a few days.

I was blessed to live with my Auntie Corrine for a year. All the memories I have of that year are so precious now. Every day she woke with a beautiful and positive light, even if things weren't perfect. She introduced me to Los Angeles, the city that she loved. We went to church together. We walked the Hollywood Walk of Fame together. We went to Venice Beach, Santa Monica, and Malibu together. We went to Trader Joe's and so many places together, but my fondest memories are just being at home with her. We watched *Wheel of Fortune* daily and competed to configure the word puzzle first. We ate freshly made kettle-style popcorn from the local farmer's market by the truckload. She made me fall in love with authentic eggplant parmigiana from her favorite Italian restaurant. We also cooked nutritious meals together. In retrospect, that's what we probably should have done instead of having carry-out that night.

But what is meant to be will be. We already loved each other, but when somebody saves your life, you will love them so much more. And I love her like she is my mother. I always will. I only wish that I would have been able to save her life in return. May she rest in peace. She is now my angel. I miss her hugs, her eyes, her smile, her laugh, her voice, her wisdom, and her love. She always hated that I smoked cigarettes. I'm sure that she is cheering for me from heaven and is happy that I quit for good and that I wrote this book. This book represents that small-but-powerful and life-saving cup of tea. I want to serve it to all people who are addicted to cigarettes. Use this to rid your body of that sick and poisonous addiction forever. I know that quitting cigarettes will be hard. But if you use all of your strength and summon all of your willpower, I also know that following the method in this book will help you quit smoking cigarettes forever and therefore help you to save your own life.

I would also like to dedicate this book to all of my brothers, sisters, and ancestors who were persecuted, enslaved, beaten, tortured, and murdered because of the color of their skin. Our ancestors dedicated their lives so that our generation could have it better and be free to pursue our dreams. Their faces, voices, stories, songs, strength, and blood are always in my heart.

Last but surely not least, I dedicate this book to President Barack Obama. In addition to reforming health care, fixing the economy, and fighting terrorists, he also managed to quit smoking cigarettes. Congratulations, Mr. President! If you can find the time to quit smoking then, "Yes, We All Can!"

CONTENTS

INTRODUCTION

Quitting cigarettes has been one of my greatest accomplishments in life. In spite of the fact that I used to love smoking, I know that I will never revert back to being a smoker because I am so happy and proud of my success. But I will tell you about my smoking days. My favorite cigarette used to be the very first one when I awoke, which gave me a nice morning buzz to start my hectic day. Also ranking high on the list were the smoke breaks after meals, with coffee, or with a glass of wine. Smoking helped me deal with stress when I was in college, which was about the time I started smoking. Now I don't even crave a cigarette, not even when I am around someone smoking one.

If I can quit smoking cigarettes, then I know that anyone can. I see people struggle to do it, and it made me want to reach out and tell the world how I was finally able to do something so difficult. If I can help at least one person to quit, then I will make a positive contribution to the world.

First of all, please know that I had plenty of false starts, so never get discouraged, even if you have tried to quit hundreds of times. Each of those failed attempts taught me about how I get tempted to smoke. This information about yourself, plus a little planning, and a lot of fun, will help you be successful on your real quit date.

The biggest lesson I learned is that truly quitting cigarettes, for life, happens in your brain. And it should begin before you actually quit smoking. You must take this process just as seriously as you take your career or an assignment for school. After all, the most precious things you possess are your health and your life.

Before you begin your journey to becoming a non-smoker, please know that this book is very informative. I have helped several people quit smoking cigarettes. However, this book will really only contribute to 10 percent of your success. The remaining 90 percent of your success will come from your commitment to doing the meditative visualization exercises, your strength, and your willpower to resist the temptation to smoke cigarettes when it arrives—and it will arrive. You already know this.

Following these steps and advice will prepare you to fight each temptation with several layers of defense techniques instead of with just one, which may have failed you in the past. You will learn to mentally prepare before you actually quit smoking; to layer up your defense tactics to fight mentally and physically; to redirect your attention and thus reduce the temptation to smoke; and to reward yourself for your accomplishments. It is a good system.

However, there may be moments when it is challenging to stick to the program. For times like these, just be prepared to turn and walk away from the temptation of smoking a cigarette. Prepare yourself to do this a thousand times. I don't believe I was tempted to smoke more than two hundred times when I was quitting. Therefore, if you are prepared to walk away from a thousand tempting situations, then you should definitely be able to walk away from, at least, hundreds. And eventually you will no longer be tempted at all.

MISSION STATEMENTS

To motivate cigarette smokers to quit cigarettes by educating them about the tobacco industry, the poisons in cigarettes, and the consequences of smoking them.

To teach cigarette smokers an effective way to quit smoking cigarettes forever, which is the method that I used. It involves nicotine therapy, meditative visualization, new experiences, and a reward system.

To inform readers of the power of meditation and its origins. To illustrate how to meditate visually to strengthen willpower and defeat psychological cigarette cravings.

To encourage the world to encourage all cigarette smokers to quit and all non-smokers to never smoke, especially the young and impressionable. To demonstrate how this strengthens the commitment to being a non-smoker forever.

NOT READY TO QUIT?
READ THIS!

According to the Centers for Disease Control and Prevention (CDC), cigarette smoking accounts for one in every five deaths in the United States every year. This is approximately 480,000 deaths per year. This is about 1,300 deaths a day. This statistic includes 201,773 female deaths and 278,544 male deaths.

Professor Sir Richard Doll, a leading cancer expert, concluded in a crude research study that every cigarette smoked deducts eleven minutes off the life of a smoker.

According to Clive Bates, the director of Action on Smoking and Health (ASH), a person who smokes twenty cigarettes a day will lose a whole day of life every week he or she continues to smoke. "As if that's not bad enough, smokers are more likely to die a more painful death and spend longer being ill while they are alive."

According to the CDC, More than sixteen million Americans suffer from cigarette-related illnesses.

Worldwide, five million people die every year, and a projected eight million will die every year by the year 2030 (CDC).

On average, smokers die ten years earlier than non-smokers (CDC).

According to current trends, about one in every thirteen young Americans alive today, age seventeen and younger, are projected to die prematurely due to tobacco-related illness. That is 5.6 million people (CDC).

Now let's talk about the cigarettes themselves. According to the CDC, every cigarette contains seven thousand chemicals.

Sixty-nine of these chemicals are known to cause cancer.

And if you think you're safe once you quit, you are wrong. You still have to motivate other smokers to quit, and if they don't or until they do, you need to stay away from their cigarette smoke. According to the CDC, fifty thousand deaths a year in the United States are caused by secondhand smoke.

Last but not least, you should consider the financial aspect of smoking cigarettes. It is very expensive. Depending on where you live, the cost of a pack of cigarettes is anywhere from five and a half to thirteen dollars. If you smoke a pack a week, you are technically spending between $286 and $676 a year just to get a buzz and kill yourself. Even if money is no issue for you, surely your life is. The next chapter will show you exactly how cigarettes affect your body.

PICTURES AND VIDEOS

Pictures to View:

I was quite surprised to know that some smokers have never seen images of how their lungs may look because of their cigarette addiction. Here are a few links to some relevant images and videos that will serve as extra motivation in your journey to quit smoking.

Smoker's Lungs vs. Non-Smoker's Lungs: http://www.rogersv.com/blog/smokers-lungs-vs-healthy-lungs/
This image shows the actual lungs of a smoker and a non-smoker. Below this image is a short video clip that compares the lung capacity of these organs during inhalation.

The Smoker's Body:
http://www.thetahealth.com/?attachment
_id=3316
This image is a collage of actual photos of head-to-toe diseases caused by smoking cigarettes.

Lungs with Emphysema:
http://www.rogersv.com/blog/smokers-lungs-vs-healthy-lungs/
These lungs are infected with emphysema. If you click the arrow on the right twice, you will see another image of a lung with emphysema that has "dirty holes" that are likely filled with tar and other poisons from cigarette inhalation.

Healthy Heart vs. Damaged Heart:
http://www.smoke-free.ca/warnings/australia-warnings.htm
This site has many pictures that are posted on cigarettes boxes in Australia. If you scroll down, you will see the hearts. The damaged heart might not look so intimidating, but the

heart attacks caused by smoking are very much so. Also, there is another picture of a lung with emphysema that has the "dirty holes."

What Happens When You Quit:
http://www.christinahuch.com/2013/06/15 -year-timeline-recovery-of-lungs-and- heart-after-quitting-smoking/
I love this image because it is the good news in this book. If you quit for good, your body will begin to heal itself immediately. This shows a fifteen-year timeline of how your body repairs itself after cigarette addiction.

Videos to Watch:

"Every Cigarette is Doing You Damage": http://m.youtube.com/watch?v=rjOZSg39 bbo
This video shows that every cigarette damages the body and demonstrates exactly how your lungs, brain, heart, and eyes are affected.

"Remove the Smoker's Lung":
https://m.youtube.com/watch?v=TAtc6qS
l1tQ

If you are sensitive to the sight of blood, then you may not want to watch this video. But it is quite motivating for smokers who are not ready to quit smoking cigarettes. It is a video of the removal of a smoker's lung. Equally impressive is this similar video, "Live Lung Surgery (Smoker's)":
https://m.youtube.com/watch?v=QwRo4v
up-3c

"Mouth Cancer Anti-Smoking Ad":
http://m.youtube.com/watch?v=MhMT5V
WB99Q

In this video, you see the effects of smoking on the mouth. A lady with mouth cancer offers some words of wisdom: "Quitting is hard. Not quitting is harder."

MINORITIES AND CIGARETTES

"We don't smoke that shit. We just sell it. We reserve the right to smoke for the young, the poor, the black, and the stupid."—R. J. Reynolds, Tobacco Company Executive

If you are a minority cigarette smoker, you have even more reason to quit because you have been specifically targeted with predatory marketing from the tobacco industry to buy and become addicted to its fatal products. Several research studies have found that these companies have promoted and advertised disproportionately higher in African American magazines, communities, and, sadly, schools. They aim directly for teens. These ruthless tobacco companies are also more likely to increase experimental smoking around minority high-school areas. They use a higher number of culturally exploitive ads and lower priced menthol cigarettes specifically to lure minorities.

They also use new cigarette products, such as the Camel Crush and Marlboro NXT (which contain a pellet that can be crushed to give a cigarette even more menthol additives), and new cigarette flavors that will psychologically appeal to minorities, such as the Caribbean Chill, Mocha Taboo, and Midnight Berry.

Tobacco companies know that minorities overwhelmingly prefer menthol cigarettes. Although no research has been published to prove that menthol cigarettes are more fatal than their non-menthol counterparts, a scientific study titled "The Preliminary Scientific Evaluation of the Possible Public Health Effects of Menthol Versus Non-menthol Cigarettes" by the Food and Drug Administration has summarized some significant findings. Their data suggests that the therapeutic properties of menthol mask the harsh physical sensations of smoking. Also, menthol use is linked to greater addiction. Menthol cigarette smokers have a stronger nicotine dependency and are less successful at quitting. Based on the FDA's evidence, they concluded that menthol cigarettes pose a higher public health risk than non-menthol cigarettes.

There is another disturbing truth that has been proven about minority cigarette smokers. According to tobaccofreekids.org, smoking rates among African Americans are lower than the national rates. However, African Americans suffer disproportionately from smoking-related illnesses. There are approximately forty-five thousand African Americans that die each year from smoking-related diseases. According to the American Lung Association, they have an increased risk for lung cancer even if they smoke the same number of cigarettes as Caucasians. On average, white men tend to consume 30 to 40 percent more cigarettes than black men, and black women consume fewer cigarettes than white women. However, black men and women are 34 percent more likely to develop lung cancer than whites.

GATHER YOUR MOTIVATION

There have always been people, moments, or things in your life that especially motivated you to quit smoking. Your attempts may not have been successful in the past, but you can still take the strength of those motivators and reuse it for this important moment, when you quit smoking cigarettes forever. But this time, you will do things a little differently. Instead of being motivated a little by one or two things, you are going to think of everything, good and bad, that will give you strength to quit. If you have the time, make a visual bulletin board of these things. If you are too busy to make a board, then at least make a presentation-worthy list. Put it somewhere you will see it every day. I recommend making several copies of your list and posting them on all the mirrors you look in, your car's dashboard, your desk at work, and your wallet. Post the list wherever you smoke and wherever you sit for long periods of time. Reflect on it often. The following is my personal list of motivators to give you some ideas.

MOTIVATORS

1. My aunties Muriel and Corrine urging me to quit smoking
2. Being a non-smoker so my kids won't smoke
3. Witnessing people struggling to breathe because of smoking
4. The healthy South Beach lifestyle
5. My aunt Marion, who died from cigarette-related cancer
6. The people who made me feel bad for being a cigarette smoker
7. The joy I feel from doing healthy things such as walking in new places with my music
8. Being healthy and happy for my family
9. The people who love me

10. My sister crying because she wanted me to quit smoking cigarettes
11. Wanting to get it done so I can start the next goal
12. Wanting to help others quit too
13. All anticigarette commercials

One particularly motivating moment in my life happened in the Bahamas. Our family vacation had come to a bittersweet end. We were at the airport taking in our final moments on the island. It was such a beautiful day, and I still remember watching the sun beginning to set. After three weeks, I still didn't want to leave. Being the aerophobe that I am, I went outside to have that last cigarette before boarding, to calm my nerves. While smoking my cigarette, I looked over and saw my mother approaching me. I wondered what she wanted because normally she would've made me come to her. As she got closer, she looked around to make sure nobody else was near.

"Give me a cigarette," she demanded.

"Huh?" I was in shock. My mother hadn't smoked a cigarette in many, many years.

"No!" I said. I would not be part of the reason she started smoking again.

"Give me a cigarette!" she demanded. "And hurry before your father sees me."

I was so disappointed. I didn't want to give her one, but she would not let up. And she is my mother. So after she demanded several times, I reluctantly reached in the pack and pulled out a cigarette.

"Just kidding," she said, smiling. "I'll never inhale that poison in my lungs again."

She then turned and sashayed away into the Bahamian sunset. And I stood there watching, with a cigarette in my mouth and a cigarette in my hand, feeling relieved and stupid at the same time. I'll never forget that. I'll never give anyone a cigarette. I'll never inhale that poison in my lungs again! And neither should you. Thanks, Mom.

VISUALIZE YOURSELF AS A NON-SMOKER FOR LIFE

There are three phases of quitting cigarettes: before you quit, when you quit, and after you quit. Each one requires planning beforehand to succeed at quitting for life. In my previous failed attempts, I used to plan to quit for good, but I never actually pictured it. I never really thought that after several months or a few years I'd have to do something to maintain my non-smoking status. But when you think of and create images of you quitting cigarettes throughout your entire life, your brain internalizes that footage, and you will find it easier to quit cigarettes forever. This practice is called visualization.

It may be hard to believe that visualization can be successful, but with practice and time, it is possible. Your brain is a powerful organ that controls your whole body. It is your built-in computer. And just like a computer, it can be programmed and reprogrammed. There are many ways to do this. In this book, we will focus on programming your brain with what I refer to as meditative visualization. It is basically a form of meditation (the act of sitting quietly in thought) in which your thoughts will be the images of your daily life as a non-smoker.

One of my older sisters first introduced me to meditation when I was very young. But for those of you who are unfamiliar with it, I will briefly try to explain meditation to you and its important role in successfully quitting cigarettes for life. According to Wikipedia, the definition of meditation is
a practice in which the individual trains
his or her mind or induces a mode of consciousness, either to realize some benefit or as an end in itself. It is a broad practice, and its earliest references can be found in the Hindu Vedas, which is a large body of

Hindu literature and scriptures originating from ancient India. The many purposes of meditation can include gaining relaxation, easing high blood pressure or depression, cultivating compassion, love, forgiveness, or a sense of well-being.

This step is so simple that it may be overlooked. But take it very seriously because this is one of the defining steps that I did during my successful quit but I didn't do during previous failed attempts. I realized that in my mind, at the time, I was a smoker. To become a non-smoker, I had to mentally change my self-perception first. Then my physical actions would correspond. You must understand that you have trained your brain for years, or for however long you have been smoking, that you are a smoker. And if you tell your brain only a few times that you are a non-smoker or that you are going to quit, your brain will eventually revert back to what it has known the most, which is smoking. However, if you tell your brain several times daily that you are a non-smoker and that you will never inhale a poisonous cigarette again and if you input the visual proof, then your brain will comply. It will begin to relay the data to the rest of your body, and your actions will follow through. Perfecting meditative visualization will take some time, practice, discipline, and commitment. In time, it will become very easy and automatic.

Here is a simple way you can begin practicing meditative visualization: When you are somewhere quiet and in a relaxed state, picture yourself going throughout your day-to-day activities without smoking. The more detailed you can picture the scene, the better. Picture yourself wanting a cigarette and then conquering that want. Picture yourself passing by hundreds of people smoking cigarettes and you keep on walking by them. You are smiling and proud that you are changing, becoming stronger, and becoming wiser. You are saving your life.

Picture your smile getting brighter as the nicotine stains disappear from your teeth. Picture everything that you love getting ten times better: coffee, tea, homemade cookies, the smell of rain, and more importantly, your inner peace.

Picture that you have just parked your car on your block after a long and stressful workday. While walking to your home, you see a young girl standing there with an unlit cigarette. She asks you for a light, and you look at her cigarette. You have a brief flashback of the high you used to get from them. You've practiced for this moment a million times in your mind. So instead of asking her for a cigarette, you look into her eyes and say your power statement for the first time: "I am a non-smoker!" You will learn more about your power statement in the following chapters. But before you walk away from that girl, you tell her that she can quit smoking just like you did. You give her this book (which you have finished and thoroughly enjoyed by now), that you just happen to have in your briefcase. Then you walk away and your day instantly feels better. Picture yourself smelling great all day and not smelling like cigarette stench. Your family and friends are proud of you. Do this every day with as many different scenarios as possible. Then visualize future life scenarios in which you are still a non-smoker, determined never to smoke again. You are proud, happy, successful, and healthier. You are determined never to smoke cigarettes again. Visualize yourself now regularly helping other smokers to quit. And now that you have successfully quit smoking cigarettes, you have moved on to your next goal. Maybe you visualize yourself starting a business, learning to play the piano, or planting a beautiful garden. Whatever it is, this is your power thought, and it is another tool for quitting cigarettes forever. You are literally programming your brain to make your body walk away from cigarettes and toward bigger and better things.

PICK A PERFECT QUIT DATE

Before you quit, there are several things to do to ensure your lifelong success as a non-smoker. Mark your quit date on your calendar. Give yourself at least a week to fully plan for success. Do not wait too long to quit, because smoking cigarettes is dangerous to your health. Pick a quit date for the morning of your day off from work to avoid stress. Do not pick a date when you are going away on vacation, because it is important to start your change as a non-smoker at the place where you spend most of your time. Post the date where you can see it all the time—on all calendars, on your phone, and on your motivation lists. Tell your family members and friends. Especially tell people with whom you smoke because it is essential to your success that you avoid being around them for at least a month. I go into further detail on this matter in the chapter "Family and Friends Who Smoke."

Memorize this date forever. This is the date you will choose to save your life. It is your second birth date.

Buy Nicotine Replacement Therapy

It is extremely important to do nicotine therapy the right way. First of all, buy it before your quit date so that you will be prepared for withdrawal symptoms. I highly recommend starting with the patch because you cannot smoke a cigarette with the patch at all, so there is no room for error. If you do decide to smoke a cigarette while wearing the patch or within a few hours of taking it off, you will get very sick from nicotine intoxication. It is a terrible nauseousness that lasts for hours. I had to learn about this the hard way. Nicotine from the patch remains in your blood for several hours after you remove it.

Make sure you pick the appropriate phase of patch based on how many cigarettes you smoke. The box of patches will indicate the number of cigarettes it is appropriate for. It is extremely important to follow the patch directions and schedule. To increase your sensitivity to the patch or any other nicotine therapy, it is recommended that you start the therapy only after refraining from cigarettes as long as you can without any nicotine assistance. This will help your body accept the new form of nicotine because it will not give a sensation as strong as that in which a toxic cigarette delivers. The patch contains only nicotine, but cigarettes have thousands of other chemicals. I went through almost two days of battling cold-turkey cravings before I put on the patch. And this is another factor that I attribute to my success.

Other methods that are helpful are nicotine gum, vaporizers (or vapes), and Chantix. However, I recommend the patch. After I used the patch for about five months, I was ready for the lowest dose of nicotine. After a couple more months on this final stage of nicotine therapy, I began to feel more secure. So I went without the patch one day and realized that I no longer needed it. That was a wonderful day. I was very proud of myself and I felt an immense sense of freedom. However, I carried around the gum to deal with surprise nicotine cravings. I may have used a couple pieces of gum per week and then I didn't even need it anymore. You will know when you are ready to stop using the patch. Most people I know took way less time than I did. But remember, it's not a race, so take as long as necessary until you are ready to stop using the patch. There are also nicotine nasal sprays and inhalers, which are available only with a doctor's prescription. Also available are Bupropion SR (Zyban) and Varenicline Tartrate (Chantix), which are non-nicotine pills.

WHAT ABOUT E-CIGARETTES, VAPES, AND MARIJUANA?

Many people find it comforting to trade their cigarette smoking habits for another smoking habit, whether it's an e-cigarette, vape, or marijuana. However, I recommend that you tackle quitting smoking cigarettes alone. When you use an e-cigarette or a vape, it is extremely easy to get sick from nicotine toxicity because you can keep smoking nonstop until the battery ends or until there's no more liquid. But it gets worse. E-cigarettes may seem harmless because they lack tobacco. But do not be fooled. These highly addictive counterparts are often unregulated and therefore may have other unhealthy ingredients, such as metal, that you will inhale into your lungs.

In 2009, the FDA detected diethylene glycol, a chemical found in antifreeze, and carcinogens called nitrosamines in some e-cigarette samples. And even if you are only inhaling pure nicotine with a vape, which is a battery-powered nicotine delivery system, there can be even more negative side effects. According to the Centers for Disease Control and Prevention, nicotine can increase the risk of sudden death by ventricular arrhythmia, which is a condition that occurs when the heart beats improperly and does not pump enough blood to the organs.

If you are going to use a vape, I recommend using an organic and nicotine free liquid. But do your research when choosing. The main ingredient, propylene glycol, has been discovered to be relatively safe through scientific research with rats and monkeys. However, greater usage can have side effects such as weight gain, dry skin, dry mouth, and increased thirst. Also, some people may be allergic to propylene glycol. People with eczema usually have a 2 percent chance of being allergic to it. People who are irritated by it can find an alternative in vegetable glycerin.

Now let's briefly talk about marijuana.
It may have its creative benefits, but according to Drugfreeworld.com, marijuana smoke has 50 to 70 percent more cancer-causing substances than cigarette smoke. One major study found that one cannabis joint can cause as much damage to the lungs as five cigarettes smoked back to back. Long-term marijuana smoking can cause bad memory, brain abnormalities, bronchitis, deformed sperm cells in men, psychosis, and it can also pass down severe hereditary defects. Medicinal marijuana, however, may not be as harmful. According to Dr. Sanjay Gupta's report on CNN, *Medical Cannabis Kills Cancer Cells and Stops Seizures*, medicinal marijuana may actually kill cancer cells. The strains of cannabis that are particularly significant with these findings are low in THC (tertahydrocannabinol), the chemical that is

responsible for its psychological effects. But it is high in CBD (cannabidiol), the chemical in marijuana that has a calming effect and is linked to killing cancer cells, relieving nausea, insomnia, and other ailments.

SWITCH UP YOUR SMOKING ROUTINE

Before you quit, switch up your smoking routine to prepare yourself to cope with the physical change of quitting smoking cigarettes forever. Gradually slowing down and changing your smoking habits will help you prepare for your quit date. For example, give up one of your routine cigarette breaks, such as your first or last one of the day. If you can do that before you actually quit, you will be well on the road to ending your addiction. Also, switching to a weaker brand of cigarettes will help. There are non-menthol and non-additive types on the market. They are not safer cigarettes, but the fact that they are not your preferred brand is the whole point. You will not enjoy smoking them as much, and therefore, you will most likely smoke less than normal.

I bought a different type of cigarette, which was a light non-menthol brand. This alone made me slow down because I didn't like the taste. It instantly made me smoke half the number of cigarettes that I normally smoked in a day. Also, I decided to give up my favorite smoking time, the morning cigarette, because I read that people who smoke first thing in the morning have a stronger addiction. In addition to this, I knew that if I gave up my favorite time to smoke ahead of my quit date, I would be somewhat ahead of the game. The night before your quit date, throw away all your ashtrays, lighters, matches, and cigarettes.

In the days leading up to your quit date, I encourage you to get into the habit of documenting the moments you are tempted to smoke. Record the time and the antecedent (what happened right before the moment you wanted the cigarette), and rate them on a scale from one to ten according to how badly you wanted to smoke a cigarette. This will teach you when and in what situations you will need the most defenses.

Use this documentation when you are meditating to visualize yourself conquering your cigarette cravings during those specific times of the day and in those specific situations. You will get stronger and stronger each time you conquer the temptation to smoke. And you will conquer your cigarette smoking habit. This will especially work if you have mastered and utilized all of the defensive counters in this book for each craving you encounter. Now that you have your essential list of motivators, you visually meditate regularly, you have some nicotine patches ready for your quit date, and you have switched up your daily routine, there are a few more tools and techniques that helped me and will help you, too. Your power thought, power statement, JOY list, and reward list will give you even more strength to stay away from cigarettes forever. Then you will be ready to help others to quit smoking cigarettes as well.

MASTER YOUR POWER THOUGHT AND POWER STATEMENT

Your power thought, and power statement, are your crucial tools to conquering your psychological cigarette cravings. That's right: You will still crave cigarettes mentally while the patch is pacifying your physical cravings. Psychological cravings are the hardest part of quitting because a patch, pill, or a vape can help cure your physical cravings, but there is no magic pill to erase the memory of cigarettes or your addiction to them. This takes mental reprogramming.

Your power thought is basically your go-to thought that you have used in your visualizations to change your mental focus from "I want a cigarette" to "I want a business." It is your most important current goal or mission. It can be anything that is extremely important and that aligns with your new non-smoking lifestyle. It might be preparing to raise money and participate in a charity run, purchasing a new car or home, becoming an inspiring artist, searching for your dream career, or improving your child's grades in school. Whatever your strongest mission is at the time, you will have to learn to focus on it whenever your thoughts shift toward cigarettes. The power thought and statement are the products of your visualization exercises, as were demonstrated in the chapter "Visualize Being a Non-Smoker for Life." Your exercises will be stronger, more active, and better able to help when you need them if you practice regularly and use them daily.

When using your power thought, be prepared to commit fully to this thought for at least twenty minutes, which is the estimated duration of a physical cigarette craving. However, all people are different, and psychological cravings are different. They can be hard to measure. Psychological cravings may be short and simple or long and seemingly endless. There were times when I had to sleep on a few of my nonstop psychological cravings. But just know that it will get easier as time goes on and as you get stronger. With practice switching the thought of a cigarette to your power thought, the duration of your psychological cravings will decrease. Eventually, they won't even be cravings, but mere quick and sometimes involuntary thoughts about your past.

It will almost be like a dress or shirt from your past that you don't wear but it's still in your closet. Maybe it is no longer in style or no longer fits, but you hold on to it because you used to like it. And whenever you go in your closet, you see it. But you know you will never wear it again. Just as you will eventually throw this outfit away and never see it again, you will eventually never consider smoking again—but only if you quit and never look back.

If you go back and forth between being a non-smoker and a smoker, then it will be very difficult to quit forever. You will have to start the whole process over and over again. The beginning is always the hardest part of quitting. The first week is especially the hardest, so be sure you are mentally prepared by practicing your meditative visualizations, your power thought, and you power statement.

Your power statement is the voicing of your power thought. It should be short and precise. In its simplest form, it should be, "I am a non-smoker! I don't smoke!" Eventually you may end up saying, "I am a CEO. I am a publisher. I am too smart to smoke! I will never smoke again. I am strong. I will win!" Recite your power statement every day, even if you only say it to yourself. Say it, believe it, and then live it.

MAKE A JOY LIST

I am sure that by now you may be asking, "Hey, where is the fun part?" Well, here it is. The key to weaning yourself off of cigarettes, successfully, is to use nicotine therapy while simultaneously preoccupying your time with fun distractions. This will help the time go by faster and therefore get you out of the rough patch of early withdrawal symptoms and smoking temptation. These distractions are more effective when they completely keep you away from any and all things that trigger you to want a cigarette. For example, if alcohol is a trigger for you, do not go to any bars, clubs, or places that serve liquor for at least three weeks. The same goes for people who are triggered by coffee. Try to avoid all coffee shops, if possible. Take a break from coffee and experiment with herbal tea. There are many excellent places to go and sample all kinds of tea. My favorite tea is Lavender mixed with Green Tea. It smells heavenly. Simply inhaling the scent of various teas offers aromatherapy benefits, in addition to the many health benefits of herbal tea. Take some time and think about all your triggers and all the things you have always wanted to do in your life but haven't. Start making this list as soon as possible so that by the time you actually quit, you will have a highly anticipated, well-thought-out, super-fun Joy list of things to do. Make your fun list as adventurous as you dare. Or you can fill it with simple things that you love to do but just don't get enough time for. The following is an example of my Joy list.

My Joy List

1. Movies
2. Barnes and Noble
3. Museums
4. Parks
5. Gym
6. Boat rides
7. Horseback Riding
8. Yoga/ Zumba
9. Drawing/ Painting
10. Charity/Volunteer
11. Cooking
12. Tennis/ Skating

I highly recommend cooking because once you quit smoking, your sense of taste multiplies, and eating delicious meals tastes like eating for the first time. Just try to keep those meals low in fat and calories because quitting smoking usually leads to a slight weight gain. However, this can be counteracted by making a commitment to a fitness plan that you enjoy and by keeping an eye on your calorie intake.

FAMILY AND FRIENDS WHO SMOKE

Just as important as finding the right things to do, is finding the right things not to do. You should not hang around other smokers for at least a month once you quit. They can either help or hurt your progress. They can help by quitting with you. They can hurt by smoking around you. Ask them if they would like to quit with you. However, be prepared to encourage them if they slip up, and tell them to encourage you if you slip up as well. But if they don't want to quit you may have to keep your distance for a while. Other than staying away from clubs and bars for about a month, I had to stay away from my friends and family members who smoke. I often try to convert them to non-smokers. They are the reason I wrote this book. However, some people just don't want to quit, aren't ready yet, or haven't read this book yet. During my preparation time, before I quit, I told them about my plans and why they wouldn't see me for a while.

It is also important to ask them, kindly, to respect your new status as a non-smoker by not smoking around you when you do spend time with them. Sometimes, it is hard for smokers to not smoke around a former smoking buddy. Remind them before you meet up that you don't want to be around cigarettes, and tell them you will only go out with them if they will not smoke around you. This is very important. When you are making plans to hang out, ask them to promise not to smoke around you. Then they will be held accountable for that promise. If they do not keep their word and light up around you, be sure to be stern with them. If they still cannot resist from lighting up, then maybe you should think twice about hanging around them until they learn to respect your health. Secondhand smoke is just as deadly as, if not deadlier than, firsthand smoke.

MAKE A REWARD LIST

The ultimate reward for quitting cigarettes is a healthier and longer life. However, I decided to reward myself even more, just because I knew all the strength that I would need to successfully quit cigarettes for life. I made a reward list for myself, and the constant mini-celebrations were just the positive reinforcement that I needed to remind myself of the ultimate reward I was giving myself. This was the most fun part of quitting cigarettes for me. It was a great motivator. Even though I was probably going to get some of these rewards anyway, getting them for this reason made the items more special to me. This is how I rewarded myself for the progress that I made. The first two days are probably the hardest. So just to make those first days easier, I planned nice small rewards for myself. Also, I planned other rewards of increasing personal value accordingly. I suggest that you post this list right next to your quit date, motivators list, and your Joy list. The following is an example of my reward list and the time sequence in which they were rewarded.

MY REWARD LIST

TIME   REWARD

TIME	REWARD
Day 1	Manicure and Pedicure
Day 2	Favorite Restaurant
Week 1	Shoes
Week 2	Purse
Month 1	Clothes
Month 2	Jewelry
Month 6	Celebration Dinner
Year 1	Party w/ Family & Friends
Year 1.5	Luggage
Year 2	Vacation

Keep in mind that this is my list and yours does not have to go by those types of rewards nor that time sequence. It's possible to make up a list of all free rewards. Also, after you have been a non-smoker for about two years, if not sooner, you shouldn't need a reward to motivate you to not smoke. But please do continue to reward yourself, occasionally, specifically for quitting smoking cigarettes because you have overcome a strong addiction and you deserve it! It is truly a great feeling. I can't wait until all of you are in a place where you know that you are never going to smoke a cigarette again. It might happen for you in a year or maybe even a month. For myself, I had that definite confidence that I would never look back after about two months.

QUIT ON YOUR QUIT DATE

YAY FOR QUIT DAY!

After all your preparation, you will be ready to quit on your quit date. Wake up, shower, turn on some motivational music, slap your nicotine patch on your shoulder (after you go cold turkey for as long as possible), and give yourself a pat on the back for taking this step onto the right path. If you feel some anxiety or melancholy, that is normal, but quickly replace any negative thoughts with positive ones. Think about your power thought and speak that power statement all day. Get ready to do all the fun stuff on your Joy list, and know that you will have a great time. Then look forward to rewarding yourself for a successful day one. You will feel like a million bucks by the end of the day, and at the end of every day that you don't smoke a cigarette. Also keep in mind all your family and friends who are rooting for you. Look at your list of motivators when times are tough. Take it with you and look at it throughout the day if necessary.

Remember that the first month is an especially fragile time for you. You know what your weaknesses are, so stay away from them, point blank. Your friends may forget about your quit date and invite you to party, but just remind them and tell them you need a month or two to yourself. If you need to socialize, spend time with your non-smoking friends and have some alcohol-free fun.

When I quit smoking cigarettes, I also quit drinking alcohol for a month. When I started drinking again, I limited myself to one glass of wine whenever I went out. This doesn't seem like much, but when you stop drinking, your tolerance level becomes lower. Thus a single glass of wine not only becomes more than enough for a night, but also falls right into the recommended dietary guidelines of beneficial intake for women, according to the National Institute of Health. For men, two glasses are allowed. The disease risks from a high alcohol intake are equally as serious as those from smoking cigarettes. Alcohol affects the brain, heart, liver, pancreas, immune system, and more. Therefore, once again, if you drink, I highly recommend taking an alcohol break while you are quitting cigarettes. It will greatly improve your chances of quitting cigarettes forever.

ONE-YEAR ANNIVERSARY!

In this phase, you have successfully gone one year without smoking cigarettes. You will realize that although you have been a non-smoker for what seems like forever, it doesn't mean that you won't still think about smoking occasionally. You may have thoughts or involuntary dreams about smoking cigarettes. You may feel sad one day and not care about being healthy anymore. You might see people smoking on TV and reminisce on how smoking once made you feel. But just know that smoking a cigarette after you have quit for a while will most likely just make you feel extremely sick.

Smoking again won't be the way you might imagine it. You will regret it and be disappointed in yourself, so just keep moving forward. Record any cigarette temptations you have in a log or a journal, and keep winning. You will realize that you are tempted and think about smoking cigarettes less and less as time goes by. To ensure your future success for the rest of your life, it will be wise for you to master your power thought and statement and use them daily. Also, instead of thinking about whether or not you will smoke a cigarette, you should switch that thought to how you can motivate other cigarette smokers to quit.

MOTIVATE OTHER SMOKERS

One way that I ensured my non-smoking status was to reinforce it daily. Whenever I saw a smoker, I became one of those people who used to annoy me by saying, "Smoking is not good for you. You should quit." But I also added, "I used to smoke. I quit. If I did it, then so can you." Then I listened to their stories and offered advice if they were willing to receive it. All those voices stayed in my head and helped me make the decision to quit. If my voice of reason gets stuck in someone else's head, then I will be happy to contribute to the next person quitting cigarettes.

According to the CDC, every day, four thousand teens smoke their first cigarette and one thousand teens become addicted and smoke daily. If you know or see teenagers who might be going through this, tell them to just say no. It may be peer pressure or curiosity that leads them to try cigarettes. However, your voice, your advice, your attention, or your caring can be the reason one person decides never to smoke. Please encourage teens and people of all ages to stay away from smoking cigarettes. It can save their lives. The best way to quit smoking cigarettes forever is to quit smoking them yourself, and then stop the cycle from repeating through another life.

FINAL TIPS

1. Most importantly, please know that one cigarette will hurt. One cigarette may seem harmless, but I have learned that one cigarette almost always means another is coming sooner or later. Once you let that strength go, it is usually gone until you get yourself together to quit again. Quit 100 percent and don't look back.

2. It is helpful to quit with someone who wants to quit, equally, as much as you do. But don't let any of his or her failed attempts, nor success, discourage your own progress.

3. Do not attempt to quit cold turkey. According to WebMD, out of all the people who quit with no nicotine therapy or medical assistance, 95 percent of them relapse.

4. Patience is a virtue. Physical cigarette cravings disappear after about five to fifteen minutes.

5. Regular exercise is a great way to reduce withdrawal symptoms and to ease the stress that may have been your reason for smoking cigarettes. It's also a good habit to pick up because quitting cigarettes can lead to a six- to ten-pound weight gain.

6. Make an empowering iPod song list or mixed CD. Listening to it when you are moody or craving a cigarette will lighten your mood and strengthen your willpower. My empowering song list includes "Superwoman" by Alicia Keys and "Run the World" by Beyoncé.

7. Do several things to keep your hands and mind occupied. Crossword puzzles, arts and crafts, volunteer work, and even regularly polishing your nails can help.

8. Get extra help from other sources:
- www.smokefree.gov
- www.cdc.gov/tobacco/quit_smoking
- www.becomeanex.org
- www.whyquit.com
- www.quitnet.com

9. Grab a great novel for your quit date. Quitting cigarettes is the perfect time to snuggle up in bed and read the latest can't-put-down book everyone is talking about. It will help you relax and provide the perfect distraction from cravings.

10. Carry a grab bag of snacks such as chopped fruit, veggies, lollipops, popcorn, and pistachios.

11. Remember, quitting cigarettes gets easier each day. So if you are having a tough day, just think about your upcoming rewards and all the fun events on your Joy list that you have scheduled. Know that the next day will be better.

12. When you feel tempted to smoke a cigarette or if you still feel like you are not ready to quit smoking, check out this video: https://m.youtube.com/watch?v=tCdOAzyKplM

13. Follow all the steps in this book. Even if some of the steps seem unnecessary, they helped me quit cigarettes forever and allowed me to help some of my loved ones to quit as well.

14. Reach out to some sort of support system if you feel like you need help or if you need to talk to people who are also going through the transition of becoming a non-smoker. Check for a local Nicotine Anonymous group that meets in your area or online.

15. If you still feel like you may need some extra help, look into therapies such as acupuncture, acupressure, or hypnosis.

Check out some of the self-hypnosis videos for quitting cigarettes on YouTube.

16. Use these apps to help you quit smoking: Get Rich or Die Smoking (Android, free) and Smoke Free (Android and iOS, free).

17. If you are not the book-reading type, subscribing to a video-on-demand service is a good idea. You can watch movies for days and seasons upon seasons of TV shows that you've never watched before. Also, there is usually a thirty-day free trial.

THANK YOU

Thank you, God, for giving me the vision of making this book. Thank you to my wonderful family and friends for all their support and inspiration, especially my mom, dad, and sisters: Joan, my inspiration for this book; Lenore, my twin; Laura, the boss; and Lorna, my fellow writer and comedienne. Thank you so much for purchasing and reading my book. I wish you the best in your journey to health, healing, and happiness. Please send any feedback, suggestions, questions, and inquiries for public speaking or book signings to:

QUITSMOKINGCIGARETTES@OUTLOOK.COM

Peace and blessings,
Nzinga Joy Burrell

Made in the USA
Monee, IL
06 November 2020